This book belongs to

....

For Jessica and her Emily bear
(who is most definitely a polar bear) K.P.

For Ben, and our endless adventures B.H.

Published in 2023 by Welbeck Childrens
An Imprint of Welbeck Children's Limited,
part of the Welbeck Publishing Group
Offices in: London-20 Mortimer Street, London WIT 3JW
& Sydney-205 Commonwealth Street, Surry Hills 2010
www.welbeckpublishing.com

Design and layout © Welbeck Children's Limited 2023
Text © 2023 Kate Peridot
Illustration © 2023 Becca Hall

A CIP record for this book is available from the Library of Congress.

ISBN 978 1 80453 511 0

Printed in Heshan, China

10 9 8 7 6 5 4 3 2 1

FSC
www.fsc.org

MIX
Paper | Supporting
responsible forestry
FSC® C020056

Meet the BEARS

KATE PERIDOT · BECCA HALL

WELBECK

So, you love bears?
Fantastic! You have great taste.
Bears are **smart**.
Bears are **curious**.
Bears are **strong**.
And they can smell you coming from miles away.

There are eight different types of bears, and they live all over the world.
To understand bears, it's best to see them in their natural habitats.
So, here are your tickets:

Pack your teddy bear and put on your boots. It's time to meet the bears.

BEAR SPOTTING KIT

flashlight

binoculars

night-vision goggles

compass

maps

bearproof lunch box

camera trap

polar gear

rain poncho

sun hat

hammock

bear-tracking handbook

HOW TO TRACK BEARS

water bottle

*My teddy is named **Bear** and he would like to meet his bear family.*

Zip up your polar onesie and look out for icebergs.
We're sailing north to the frozen sea to meet a bear who loves the cold.
BEWARE. This bear's fur is the same color as the snow so they can sneak up
on their favorite prey-seals-or anything else that smells like dinner.

Meet the POLAR BEAR.

He sees well in daylight and in the dark.

He has small ears so they don't get cold, but he can still hear whale song and seals calling beneath the ice.

The polar bear is the largest bear. He can sniff prey resting on the ice 20 miles away and he'll swim from ice floe to ice floe to hunt them.

🐾 **FOOD:**

seals

walrus

beluga whales

fish

eggs

birds

reindeer

🐾 **FUR:**
Blubbery black skin beneath two layers of pale translucent fur which absorbs and traps heat.

🐾 **RANGE:**
Across the Arctic Circle—Alaska, Greenland, northern Canada, Russia, and Norway.

🐾 **HIBERNATE:**
No, but moms dig snow-dens to have cubs.

Those turned-in broad furry paws and short curved claws help him grip the ice and dig in the snow.

Is your teddy a *polar bear*?

No. He doesn't have white fur.

We swoop down and land at the mouth of a tumbling river.
We're in luck. This bear loves to fish and it's the start of salmon season.
She's with her cubs and will be very protective, so stay well out of her
way and use your binoculars.

Meet the BROWN BEAR.

Her fuzzy ears are always alert
to the sounds in the forest.
She'll avoid you if she can.

She has a shoulder
hump of muscle to
help her dig deep
winter dens.

Those long-curved
claws are great tools
for digging up tasty
roots and shifting
earth.

🐾 **FOOD:**

roots

berries

plants

fish

Insects

🐾 **FUR:**

Brown with flecks of blond or black.

🐾 **HIBERNATE:**

Yes, from October to March.

🐾 **RANGE:**

There are 15 different types of brown bear, including the grizzly bear. Brown bears roam parts of North America, Russia, the Middle East, Europe, and Japan.

Her sense of smell is one of the best in the animal kingdom. It tells her who's in the forest and where that delicious scent is coming from.

Is your teddy a brown bear?

No. He doesn't have brown fur.

She can run up to 35 mph, much faster than the fastest person.

We have been on a day-long hike, winding up through a tall pine forest. We're ready to set up camp, eat dinner, and wriggle into our sleeping bags. **CRASH. Uh-oh!** An evening raider has entered the camp and he's eating our breakfast and lunch. Someone forgot to close their bearproof lunch box!

Meet the BLACK BEAR.

TRAIL THIS
WAY →

He is intelligent and not as fearful of people as other bears. He'll break into a trash can or smash a parked car window to swipe a snack.

He has short fur and rounded ears.

🐾 FOOD:

insects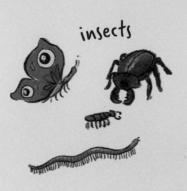

nuts

fruits

 small animals

anything he can get his paws on

FUR:
Black to dark brown. Kermode bears and glacier bears are rare subspecies of black bear and have creamy-white or silvery-blue fur.

HIBERNATE:
Yes. Between November and April.

RANGE:
Mountains and forests across North America.

His favorite place is up a tree, which is where he goes when he's frightened or if he needs to take a nap.

In the autumn, he looks for a place to hibernate which could be a cave or even beneath someone's house!

No. He has a long fur coat.

Is your teddy a black bear?

After an uncomfortable day riding a llama up a steep mountain path you dismount and we follow an animal track into the cloud forest. This bear is shy and hard to find, so use your guidebook to identify her pawprints and poo, and don't forget to look up! This bear loves to spend time in the tree canopy. *SNAP. CRACK.*

Meet the SPECTACLED BEAR.

She has a shorter nose
than other bears.

Her front legs are longer than
her back legs to help her climb.

She builds tree nests from broken branches to sleep on and to use as a platform to pick fruit.

The light-colored fur around her eyes looks like she is wearing a pair of glasses.

🐾 FOOD:

bulbs

berries

small animals

cactus flowers

plants

🐾 FUR:
Black to reddish brown.

🐾 HIBERNATE:
No. The climate is warm and plenty of food grows all year round.

🐾 RANGE:
The forest slopes of the Andean Mountains in South America.

Is your teddy a *spectacled* bear?

No. He doesn't have spectacles.

It's a hot, bumpy ride through the tinder-dry forest. The driver breaks suddenly and points to a pile of bear poo on the ground. We tiptoe on foot to a clearing where a shaggy-coated animal, with his head in a termite nest, is noisily sucking up insects. *Shluuuurp.*

Meet the SLOTH BEAR.

He has a light-colored snout and V or Y shaped markings on his chest.

His long fur protects him from insect bites and stings.

🐾 FOOD:

honey

fruit

insects

He has very long claws, perfect for digging ants and termites out of their nests.

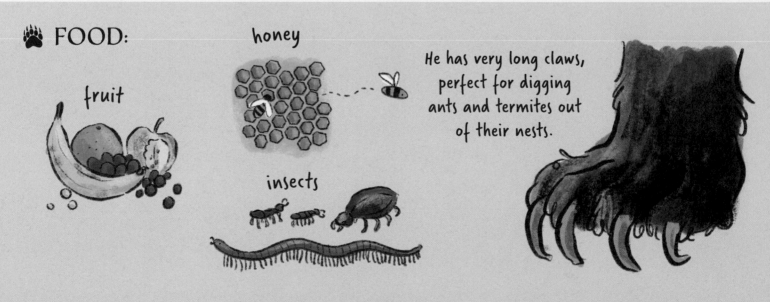

FUR:
Long jet-black fur.

HIBERNATE:
No. The climate is warm and plenty of food grows all year round.

RANGE:
The sloth bear lives in the jungles, dry forests, and tall grasslands of India, Nepal, and Sri Lanka.

He will climb a tree to knock a beehive to the ground.

Is your teddy a sloth bear?

No. He doesn't have long claws.

He can close his nostrils and suck up insects like a vacuum cleaner through a gap in his front teeth.

The river meanders through the jungle like a brown snake. It's so hot and humid we stop to glug water and spot bear pawprints in the mud on the bank. The bear might come back so we decide to moor up and make a hide out of branches. At dawn, we're woken by the sound of claws scratching on tree bark.

Meet the SUN BEAR.

She is named after the pale orange markings on her chest which look a bit like the rising or setting sun.

Her short fur repels the heavy tropical rain.

The sun bear is the smallest bear.

She tears off bark with her curved claws and uses her very long 8-inch tongue to root out tasty insects or honey from beehives.

FOOD:

insects

rodents

honey

fruit

She is an expert climber and spends most of her time in the tree canopy where she makes nests to sleep.

FUR:
Very short dark brown to black fur.

HIBERNATE:
No. The climate is warm and there is plenty of food all year round.

RANGE:
Dry forests and rain forests, from eastern India to southern China, and down to Borneo.

*Is your teddy a **sun bear**?*

No. He doesn't have a long tongue.

We land on a plateau in the Tibetan mountains and hike up through the forest to the snow line. All around, tall bamboo grows beneath ancient fir trees. Suddenly the guide waves us behind a tree. A female bear follows her cub out of a den, their black and white fur perfectly matching the forest shadows and patches of snow.

Meet the GIANT PANDA.

She has strong jaws to crunch through tough bamboo.

She has a specially-adapted second thumb to grip bamboo and she's a great climber.

🐾 FUR:
Distinctive black and white markings.

🐾 HIBERNATE:
No, but moms make dens out of branches when they are expecting cubs.

🐾 RANGE:
Fir and bamboo forests on six isolated mountain ranges in China.

🐾 FOOD:
Mostly bamboo. They spend up to 16 hours a day eating.

Due to their high fiber diet, they can poo up to 40 times a day!

She sometimes climbs a tree backward with hind legs in the air, like a handstand and sprays a smelly pee to tell other pandas, "Keep out! This is my territory!".

*Is your teddy a **panda**?*

No. He doesn't have a white face.

It's taken days to track this elusive bear. We climb a steep, narrow mountain path with death-defying drops. Just before sunset we reach a plateau where nut trees grow and set up the camera trap. It's best to wait downwind–this bear doesn't like surprises. At dusk a family of bears amble out of the forest, climb a tree, and shake nuts on to the forest floor to eat. **CLICK. CLICK.**

Meet the MOON BEAR.

He is named after the whitish-yellow moon-shaped markings on his chest and he has a distinctive fur ruff.

Adult bears have been spotted caring and playing with their cubs. In other bear species, only moms stay with cubs. This makes the moon bear the most sociable and playful of all the bears.

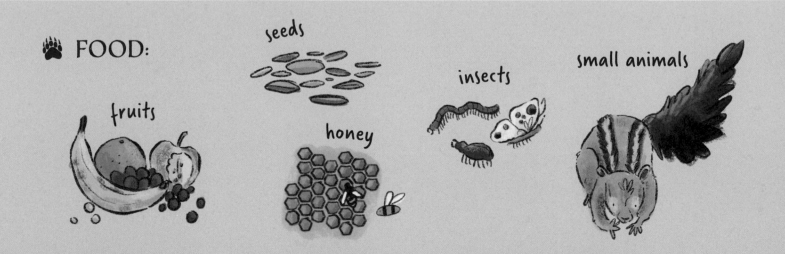

🐾 FOOD:

seeds

fruits

honey

insects

small animals

FUR:
Black fur with longer fur like a mane around the neck.

HIBERNATE:
only in northern regions of their habitat.

RANGE:
Remote heavily-forested mountainous areas of Siberia, Pakistan, China, Korea, Taiwan, Japan, and southern Asia.

He roams great distances to find seasonal food and prefers to forage at dawn and dusk. During the day, he snoozes in a tree, sometimes making a nest there.

Is your teddy a moon bear?

Yes. He is a moon bear and he's excited to meet his bear family.

So you've met all eight bears and discovered which family your teddy bear belongs to. Now it's time to head home and share your knowledge and photos with your other teddy bears.

Perhaps you can help them to discover their bear families too!

Did you know that some animals that are called bears are not bears?

Meet the RED PANDA

The red panda is a panda but not a bear. In fact, the red panda is the original panda. The giant panda was discovered and named by zoologists much later. Both pandas eat lots of bamboo and their habitats overlap, so naturally people thought they were related. Scientists have since discovered red pandas are a species all on their own. A red panda is about the same size as a pet cat. He has a long bushy tail which helps him balance.

RANGE:
Eastern Himalayan Mountains of China, Nepal, Bhutan, and northern Myanmar.

Meet the KOALA

The word "koala" comes from the aboriginal language of Australia and means "no drink". Koalas don't come down from their trees to drink from rivers or pools. They take in water from the enormous amounts of eucalyptus leaves they eat. When the first Australian settlers landed in ships, they added the word bear, but we now know koalas are more closely related to kangaroos and wombats.

RANGE:
Eucalyptus forests of eastern and southeastern Australia.

Meet the BEARCAT

The bearcat is not a bear or a cat. He belongs to the civet and mongoose family, but you can see why people thought he might be a bear. He has bear-like fur and walks like a bear but he has a long tail that helps him to balance and grip branches. He also has white whiskers to feel his way around the forest at night, a bit like a cat.

RANGE:
Tropical forests of south-east Asia.

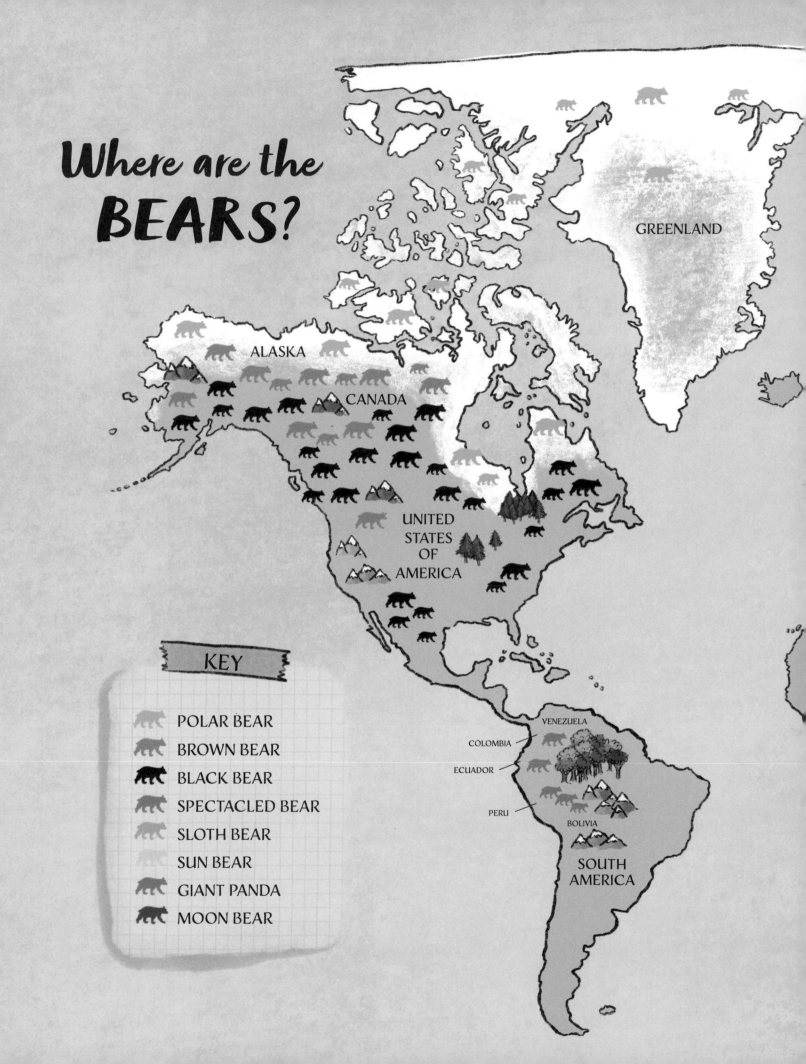

Where are the BEARS?

GREENLAND

ALASKA

CANADA

UNITED
STATES
OF
AMERICA

VENEZUELA
COLOMBIA
ECUADOR
PERU
BOLIVIA

SOUTH
AMERICA

KEY

POLAR BEAR

BROWN BEAR

BLACK BEAR

SPECTACLED BEAR

SLOTH BEAR

SUN BEAR

GIANT PANDA

MOON BEAR

ARCTIC CIRCLE

SIBERIA

RUSSIA

EUROPE

CHINA

JAPAN

INDIA

AFRICA

AUSTRALIA

Sizing up the BEARS

Average measurements of male bears
in order of shoulder height

45.5in

Average 6-year-old

SUN BEAR

Length: 4ft 5in
Shoulder Height: 2ft 3.5in
Standing Height: 4ft 11in

GIANT PANDA

Length: 5ft 1in
Shoulder Height: 2ft 5.5in
Standing Height: 5ft 5in

SPECTACLED BEAR

Length: 5ft 5in
Shoulder Height: 2ft 7.5in
Standing Height: 5ft 9in

SLOTH BEAR

Length: 5ft 7in
Shoulder Height: 2ft 8.5in
Standing Height: 5ft 11in

BLACK BEAR

Length: 5ft 3in
Shoulder Height: 2ft 9.5in
Standing Height: 5ft 9in

MOON BEAR

Length: 5ft 3in
Shoulder Height: 3ft 1in
Standing Height: 5ft 7in

BROWN BEAR

Length: 7ft 5.6in
Shoulder Height: 3ft 11in
Standing Height: 8ft 2.5in

POLAR BEAR

Length: 8ft 10in
Shoulder Height: 4ft 9in
Standing Height: 9ft 4in

How to stay safe in
BEAR COUNTRY

🐾 Walk in a group and look out for signs a bear is nearby.

🐾 Bears don't like surprises so make lots of noise by stomping and talking on the trail. They will smell and hear you before you see them.

🐾 When camping, put food, including dishes, cutlery, and pans, in a bearproof box or hang them high in a tree from a thin branch away from camp so bears are not tempted.

🐾 If you come across a bear unexpectedly, don't run away. The bear may think you're prey. Bears run, swim, and climb faster than you can!

🐾 Talk calmly to the bear and raise your arms to look bigger, and slowly move out of the way.

🐾 If a bear stands up on its hind legs, it's not being threatening, it's curious. The bear is trying to catch your scent and get a better look at you.

🐾 A bear will only charge at someone if:
- the bear is surprised, and you are too close
- a mother bear feels she must protect her cubs
- a bear feels it must defend its food
- a bear is very hungry

🐾 To make an angry or hungry bear back away, stand together and stand your ground. Make yourselves look as big as possible and make lots of noise. Bears hate loud noises!

🐾 Polar bears are the most dangerous bear. People who live in the Arctic Circle must be very careful.

🐾 To go bear-spotting, always follow an expert guide who understands bear behavior and keep a safe and respectful distance.

TO LEARN MORE ABOUT BEARS
The International Association for Bear Research and Management (IBA):
https://www.bearbiology.org/bears-of-the-world/

World Wildlife Fund for Nature: https://www.wwf.org.uk

Born Free: https://www.bornfree.org.uk